R. A. TORREY
on the
HOLY SPIRIT
A 30-DAY DEVOTIONAL TREASURY

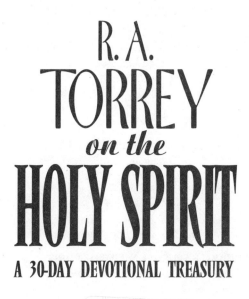

D0062591

Compiled and Edited by
LANCE WUBBELS

Emerald Books

P.O. Box 635
Lynnwood, WA 98046

OTHER CHRISTIAN LIVING CLASSICS

30-DAY DEVOTIONAL TREASURIES

Charles Finney on Spiritual Power
George Müller on Faith
Andrew Murray on Holiness
Hudson Taylor on Spiritual Secrets
Charles Spurgeon on Prayer
R. A. Torrey on the Holy Spirit

CHARLES SPURGEON: BELIEVER'S LIFE SERIES

Grace Abounding in a Believer's Life
A Passion for Holiness in a Believer's Life
The Power of Prayer in a Believer's Life
Spiritual Warfare in a Believer's Life
The Triumph of Faith in a Believer's Life
What the Holy Spirit Does in a Believer's Life

CHARLES SPURGEON: LIFE OF CHRIST SERIES

The Power of Christ's Miracles
The Power of Christ's Prayer Life
The Power of Christ's Second Coming
The Power of Christ's Tears
The Power of Christ the Warrior
The Power of the Cross of Christ

F. B. MEYER: BIBLE CHARACTER SERIES

The Life of Abraham: The Obedience of Faith
The Life of David: Shepherd, Psalmist, King
The Life of Joseph: Beloved, Hated, Exalted
The Life of Moses: The Servant of God
The Life of Paul: A Servant of Jesus Christ
The Life of Peter: Fisherman, Disciple, Apostle

R. A. Torrey on the Holy Spirit
Copyright © 1998 by Lance Wubbels

Published by Emerald Books
P.O. Box 635
Lynnwood, WA 98046

Unless otherwise noted, Scripture quotations in this book are taken from the Holy Bible, New International Version®, Copyright© 1973, 1978, 1984 by the International Bible Society. Used by permission of Zondervan Publishing House.

ISBN 1-883002-48-6

Printed in the United States of America.

INTRODUCTION

Reuben Archer Torrey (1856–1928) was both an evangelist and a Bible scholar. Long associated with D. L. Moody, he became most prominent during world preaching tours in 1902 and 1921, which took him to China, Japan, Australia, New Zealand, India, Germany, and the United Kingdom. His preaching in Wales in 1902 has been noted as one of the causes of the Welsh revivals of the early 1900s. He was the first superintendent of the Moody Bible Institute and wrote numerous devotional and theological books.

Spiritual awakening followed R. A. Torrey throughout his career as an evangelist. In revivals with the popular gospel singer Charles W. Alexander, Dr. Torrey filled meeting halls with his magnetic presence, passion, and earnestness.

About his own ministry, Torrey said, "It was a great turning point when after much thought and study and meditation I became satisfied that the baptism with the Holy Spirit was an experience for today and for me, and set myself to obtain it.

"While a great deal is said in these days concerning the baptism with the Holy Spirit, I am afraid that there are many who talk about it and pray for it who have no clear and definite idea of what it is. But the Bible, if carefully studied, will give us a view of this wondrous blessing that is perfectly clear and remarkably definite."

Lance Wubbels, compiler and editor

THE PERSONALITY OF THE HOLY SPIRIT

—◢◣◥—

May the grace of the Lord Jesus Christ,
and the love of God, and the fellowship of
the Holy Spirit be with you all.
—2 Corinthians 13:14

It is impossible to understand the work of the Holy Spirit, or to get into a right relationship with the Holy Spirit, without first coming to know the Holy Spirit as a Person. One of the most fruitful sources of error and misconception, of unwholesome enthusiasm and false fire and fanaticism, in the treatment of this whole subject, is from trying to know the work of the Holy Spirit before we first come to know the Holy Spirit himself.

The doctrine of the personality of the Holy Spirit is of the highest importance from the standpoint of worship. If the Holy Spirit is thought of as an impersonal influence or power, as so many do, then we rob Him of the worship that is His due, of the love that is His due, and of the faith and confidence and surrender and obedience and worship that are

His due. I pause to ask you, "Do you worship the Holy Spirit?" It is one thing to theoretically acknowledge the Holy Spirit in the doxology, "Praise Father, Son, and Holy Spirit." It is quite another thing to realize the meaning and the force of these words.

It is of the highest importance from a practical standpoint that we know the Holy Spirit as a Person. To think of the Spirit as merely an influence or power, then your thought will constantly be, "How can I get hold of the Holy Spirit and use it? How can I get more of the Holy Spirit?" But if you think of Him in the biblical way, as a Person of divine majesty and glory, your thought will be, "How can the Holy Spirit get hold of me and use me? How can the Holy Spirit get more of me?"

If you think of the Spirit as an influence that you are to get hold of, and then believe you have received the Spirit, the inevitable result will be that you will strut around as if you belonged to a superior order of Christians. We see far too much of that today. If you think of the Spirit as a divine Person of infinite majesty, who comes to dwell in our hearts and take possession of us and use us as He wills, it leads to humility. No great biblical truth more efficiently puts one in the dust and keeps one in the dust than this.

—◦∾◦—

Heavenly Father, open my eyes to see the Holy Spirit as a Person Who is just as real as Your Son Jesus. Show me what it is about the Spirit that I have misunderstood. There is nothing I desire more than to come to know Him as He really is. Amen.

MORE THAN
AN INFLUENCE

———✦✦✦———

*And do not grieve the Holy Spirit of God, with whom
you were sealed for the day of redemption.*
—Ephesians 4:30

The first line of proof of the personality of
the Holy Spirit is that all the distinctive char-
acteristics of personality are ascribed to the
Holy Spirit. They are knowing, feeling, and
willing. Any being who knows and feels and
wills is a person.

"For who among men knows the thoughts
of a man except the man's spirit within him?
In the same way no one knows the thoughts
of God except the Spirit of God" (1 Cor. 2:11).
Here *knowledge* is ascribed to the Holy Spirit.
The Holy Spirit is not a mere illumination that
enlightens and strengthens our minds to see
truth that we would not otherwise discover.
No, the Holy Spirit is a Person who knows the
things of God and reveals to us what He Himself knows.

"All these are the work of one and the
same Spirit, and he gives them to each one,

just as he determines" (1 Cor. 12:11). Here the Holy Spirit is presented as a divine Person who gets hold of us and uses us according to His will. Yet countless sincere believers are going astray by trying to get hold of some divine power that they can use according to their will. What an evil thought that I might grasp divine power and use it in my foolishness and ignorance! Such is not the way. But I rejoice that there is a divine Person who can capture my heart and use me according to His infinitely wise and loving will.

"And he who searches our hearts knows the mind of the Spirit, because the Spirit intercedes for the saints in accordance with God's will" (Rom. 8:27). Note here that the Greek word for *mind* comprehends all three ideas of knowledge, feelings, and will. It is the same word as "the sinful mind is hostile to God" (Rom. 8:7), where the thought comprehends the whole moral and intellectual life of the flesh in hostility against God.

Every biblical reference to the Holy Spirit speaks of a divine Person who thinks, feels, and wills. May we so value His presence that we never grieve His infinite heart.

—————

Holy Spirit, I confess that I have often failed to recognize and honor You, and I know that I have often missed out on the work that You desire to do in and through my life. Help me to treat You as real as I would Jesus if He were beside me physically. Amen.

THE LOVING SPIRIT

—⟨∿∿∿⟩—

*Then the LORD said, "My Spirit will
not contend with man forever."*
—Genesis 6:3

I urge you, brothers, by our Lord Jesus Christ
and by the love of the Spirit, to join me in my
struggle by praying to God for me" (Rom.
15:30). The Holy Spirit is not a mere blind
power, no matter how beneficent, that comes
into our hearts and lives, but is Himself a
divine Person, loving us with the tenderest
love. Such a wonderful thought!

Do you ever kneel down and look up to
the Holy Spirit and say, "Holy Spirit, I thank You
for Your great love for me"? And yet we owe
our salvation as truly to the love of the Spirit
as we do to the love of the Father and the love
of the Son. If it had not been for the love of
God the Father, looking down upon me in my
lost state, yes, anticipating my fall and ruin
and sending His own Son down to this world
to die upon the cross in my place, I would be

a lost man today. If it had not been for the love of Jesus Christ coming down to this world in obedience to the Father, and laying down His life, a perfect atoning sacrifice on the cross of Calvary in my behalf, I would be a lost man today.

But if it had not been for the love of the Holy Spirit to me, leading Him to come down to this world in obedience to the Father and the Son, to seek me out in my lost condition, following me day after day, and week after week, and month after month, following me when I would not listen to Him, when I deliberately turned my back upon Him, when I insulted Him, following me into places where it must have been agony for that Holy One to go, until at last He succeeded in bringing me to my senses and bringing me to realize my utterly lost condition, and revealing the Lord Jesus to me as just the Savior whom I needed, and induced me and enabled me to receive the Lord Jesus as my Savior and Lord; if it had not been for this patient, long-suffering, never-wearying love of the Spirit of God to me, I would be a lost man today.

—❧—

Yes, I gladly come to give You thanks, dear Spirit of God, for contending with me and for not giving up on me when I would not hear the voice of God and bow my knee to the Savior's love. How deeply I must have grieved and angered You. But Your love overwhelmed me as You showed me the sacrifice of Jesus. Praise Your name. Amen.

THE INDWELLING
HOLY ONE

―――∽∾∽―――

*"You gave your good Spirit to instruct them. You did
not withhold your manna from their mouths, and
you gave them water for their thirst."*
—Nehemiah 9:20

Here in Nehemiah both intelligence and goodness are ascribed to the Holy Spirit. There are those who say that the personality of the Holy Spirit is in the New Testament but not in the Old Testament, but this is hardly the case. This verse also clearly indicates the doctrine of the trinity which some claim as not being in the Old Testament. In actual fact the doctrine of the trinity is found hundreds of times in the Old Testament.

"And do not grieve the Holy Spirit of God, with whom you were sealed for the day of redemption" (Eph. 4:30). Here *grief* is ascribed to the Holy Spirit. In other words, the Holy Spirit is not a mere impersonal influence or power that dwells in your heart and mine. No, He is a Person, a Person who loves us, a Person who is holy and intensely sensitive against sin, a Person who recoils from sin in what we would call its slightest forms as the holiest person on earth never recoiled from sin in its grossest and most repulsive forms. And He sees whatever we do, hears whatever we say, sees our every thought; and if there is anything impure, unholy, immodest, uncharitable, untrue, false, censorious, bitter, or unChristlike in any way, in word or thought or act, He is grieved beyond expression. This is a wonderful thought, and it is to me the mightiest incentive that I know for a careful walk, a walk that will please this indwelling Holy One in every act and word and thought.

Bearing this thought of the Holy Spirit in our mind will help us to solve all the questions and gray areas that perplex our day. If there is any question about whether an action we are about to take is right or wrong, we need only to consider that if we go, the Holy Spirit will go, too, for He dwells in our heart. Are we going to a place or thinking a thought that is congenial to the Holy Spirit? If not, let us stop it immediately.

—————

Father God, I marvel at the infinite personalities of Your Son and of Your Spirit. But if these words that I understand with my mind are going to make a difference in my life, they must penetrate my inner heart. Breathe Your life into me and change me, Lord. Amen.

THE SPIRIT OF TRUTH

—◊◊◊—

But God has revealed it to us by
his Spirit. The Spirit searches all things,
even the deep things of God.
—1 Corinthians 2:10

The second line of proof of the personality of the Holy Spirit is that many actions ascribed to the Spirit are ones that only a person can do. Paul tells the Corinthians that the Spirit is far more than an a mere illumination to our minds concerning truth, He is a Person who searches into the deep things of God and reveals to us the thing that He discovers.

"In the same way, the Spirit helps us in our weakness. We do not know what we ought to pray for, but the Spirit himself intercedes for us with groans that words cannot express" (Rom. 8:26). Here the Holy Spirit is represented as doing what only a person can do, that is, praying. He is not merely an influence that comes upon us and impels us to pray, nor is He a mere guidance to us in offering our prayers. No, the Holy Spirit is praying for us and through us down here on earth.

"But the Counselor, the Holy Spirit, whom the Father will send in my name, will teach you all things and will remind you of everything I have said to you" (John 14:26). Here the Holy Spirit is represented as doing what only a person can do, namely, teaching. We have the same thought in John 16:12–14: "I have much more to say to you, more than you can now bear. But when he, the Spirit of truth, comes, he will guide you into all truth. He will not speak on his own; he will speak only what he hears, and he will tell you what is yet to come. He will bring glory to me by taking from what is mine and making it known to you." Again the Holy Spirit is represented as a living, personal teacher to us.

Every time we study our Bible it is possible to have this divine Person, the author of the Book, to interpret it to us, and to teach us its real and innermost meaning. It is a precious thought. How often have we thought that if only we could hear some great human teacher, we could make some progress in our spiritual life. But listen, we can have a teacher more competent by far than the greatest human teacher who ever spoke on earth for our teacher every day, and that peerless teacher is the Holy Spirit.

—◦◦◦—

Holy Spirit, I never imagined the depth of involvement that You desire to have in my life. I bow before You and ask that You might be the teacher of my heart and mind. Take the Word of God and make it real in my life. Amen.

ANOTHER COUNSELOR

━━∽∾∿━━

"But I tell you the truth: It is for your good that I am going away. Unless I go away, the Counselor will not come to you; but if I go, I will send him to you."
—John 16:7

The third line of proof of the personality of the Holy Spirit is that an office is predicated of the Holy Spirit that could only be predicated of a person. Look, for example at John 14:16–17: "And I will ask the Father, and he will give you another Counselor to be with you forever—the Spirit of truth. The world cannot accept him, because it neither sees him nor knows him. But you know him, for he lives with you and will be in you." Here the Holy Spirit is represented as *another Counselor* who is coming to take the place of our Lord Jesus. Up to this time our Lord Jesus had been the friend always at hand to help the disciples in every emergency that arose. But now He is going, and He tells them that though He is going another is coming to take His place. Can you for a moment imagine our Lord Jesus saying this if the other who is coming to take His place were a mere impersonal influence or power? No! No! What our Lord said was that He, one divine Person, was going, but that another Person, just as divine as He, was coming to take His place.

I take this as one of the most precious promises in the Word of God: that another Person just as divine as Jesus, just as loving and tender and strong to help, is by my side always, yes, dwells in my heart every moment to commune with me and to help me in every emergency that can possibly arise. The Greek word for "Counselor" is *parakletos,* which means "one called to stand alongside another"; one called to take his part and help him in every emergency that arises. Just like Jesus, the Holy Spirit is with us wherever we go, every hour of the day or night, always at our side.

What a precious and wondrous thought. If this thought gets into your heart and stays there, you will never have another moment of fear as long as you live. How can we fear under any circumstances if we really believe that He is by our side? How can loneliness or a broken heart remain? Do you know this Friend, the Holy Spirit?

———

Lord Jesus, how can I thank You enough for sending the Holy Spirit to be my Counselor? I take this precious thought into my heart and ask You to unveil its meaning. I truly need You, Holy Spirit, to be at my side every hour of the day and night. Amen.

DAY 7

HOLY SPIRIT CONVICTION

———〜〜〜———

*"When he comes, he will convict the world of guilt
in regard to sin and righteousness and judgment."*
—John 16:8

It is the work of the Holy Spirit to convict people of sin in such a way as to produce a deep
sense of personal sinfulness. This is where the
work of salvation begins in most people: they
are brought to realize that they are sinners
and that they need a Savior, and then they are
ready without much urging to accept Jesus
Christ, when He is presented to them as the
all-sufficient Savior they so sorely need.

One of the great needs of the present day
is conviction of sin. Men and women have no
realization of the awfulness of sin or of their
standing before God. We are very sharp-
sighted as regards the sins and shortcomings
of others, but very blind to our own. "The heart
is deceitful above all things and beyond cure"
(Jer. 17:9). And the world is so blind to its sinfulness that no one but the Holy Spirit can

ever convince the world of sin, bringing men to see how sinful they are. Neither you nor I can convince any man of sin, even with the most persuasive reasoning and powerful stories. We may get men to cry by a moving story, but mere shedding of tears over emotional stories and touching songs is not conviction of sin. Real conviction of sin can only be produced by the Holy Spirit.

But while it is utterly impossible for us to convince men of sin, the Holy Spirit can do it. And, if we put ourselves at the disposal of the Holy Spirit for Him to use us as He will, and if we would look to the Holy Spirit to convince men of sin through us, and if we would be more careful to be in such relations with God that the Holy Spirit can work through us, we would see far more conviction of sin.

The Holy Spirit can convict men as powerfully today as He did on the Day of Pentecost when three thousand men and women were cut to their hearts (Acts 2:37). If Peter had preached the same sermon the day before the Holy Spirit came, there would have been no such results. Oh, we need to believe in the Holy Spirit's power to convict men of sin, and we need to trust Him to do His glorious work through us.

—✹—

Holy Spirit, we live in a world that is frighteningly desensitized to the awfulness of sin. I ask You to start in my own life, to search me and show me my heart as regards sin. Make me a light that You can shine through to others. Amen.

WHERE CONVICTION IS NEEDED

---≈∾≈---

*"In regard to sin, because men do not believe
in me; in regard to righteousness, because I
am going to the Father, where you can see me no
longer; and in regard to judgment, because the
prince of this world now stands condemned."*
—John 16:9–11

The sin of which the Holy Spirit convicts men and women is the sin of unbelief in Jesus Christ, not in the endless list of other sins. This was the sin of which the Holy Spirit convicted the three thousand on the Day of Pentecost (Acts 2:36–37). When they realized they had rejected the Lord and Christ, they were cut to their hearts. This awful sin is the very sin of which it is most difficult to convince proud and arrogant men. But when the Spirit of God comes to a man, he does not look upon unbelief in Jesus Christ as a mark of intellectual superiority or excuse it behind an inherent inability to believe. While he may bitterly regret his dishonesty or his impurity or whatever other sins he may be guilty, he sees and feels that the most awful of his sins is the sin of rejecting the glorious Son of God.

The Holy Spirit also convicts the world of righteousness; not of our righteousness, for we have none, but of Jesus Christ's righteousness, attested by His resurrection from the dead and by His ascension to the Father. The convicted sinner needs to see the righteousness that God has provided for him in Christ, and only the Holy Spirit can bring this to him.

The third thing that the Holy Spirit convicts men about is judgment, attested by the judgment of the prince of this world, the devil. There has perhaps never been a day in the whole history of the church when the world needed more to be convinced of judgment than today. The average man has almost no knowledge of a future judgment, and the church has largely lost all realization of future judgment and of a future awful hell. Only the Holy Spirit can bring this revelation of the infinite majesty and glory of Jesus Christ, and such a revelation of the awfulness of sin and to the future eternal destiny of those who would not accept Jesus Christ.

Lord Jesus, without an outpouring of Your Spirit this world will remain blinded to sin and righteousness and judgment. In most places these are never considered, or if they are, they are disdained. Shine on Your church in power and truth. Amen.

A TRUE KNOWLEDGE OF JESUS

—◦◦◦—

*"When the Counselor comes, whom
I will send to you from the Father, the Spirit of
truth who goes out from the Father, he will testify
about me. And you also must testify, for you
have been with me from the beginning."*
—John 15:26–27

It is the work of the Holy Spirit to bear witness concerning Jesus Christ. All the work of the Holy Spirit centers in Jesus Christ. It is His work to magnify Christ to us, to glorify Christ by taking of the things of Christ and declaring them to us.

It is only through the direct testimony of the Holy Spirit in the individual heart that any man ever comes to a true and saving knowledge of Jesus Christ (1 Cor. 12:3). No amount of listening to the testimony of men regarding Jesus Christ, and no amount even of studying what the Scriptures say about Christ, will ever lead anyone to the knowledge of Jesus Christ unless the Holy Spirit, the living Spirit of God, takes the message of men, or the testimony of the written Word, and interprets it directly to our hearts.

It is true that the Holy Spirit's testimony regarding Jesus Christ is found in the Bible. In fact, that is exactly what the whole Bible is, the Holy Spirit's testimony to Jesus Christ. But the Holy Spirit must take His own testimony as it is found in the Word of God and interpret it directly to the heart of the individual and make it a living thing in his heart, or he will not come to a saving knowledge of Jesus Christ.

If you wish men to get such a true view of Jesus Christ that they will believe in Him, you must seek for them the testimony of the Holy Spirit, and you must put yourself in such relations to God that the Holy Spirit can bear His testimony through you. No amount of argument and persuasion will ever bring anyone to know Jesus Christ.

And if you wish to have a true knowledge of Jesus Christ yourself, it is not enough that you study the Word and what the Spirit of God has said about Jesus Christ in the Word: you must seek for yourself the testimony of the Spirit of God directly to your own heart through His Word, and put yourself in such relations to God that the Holy Spirit can bear His testimony directly to your heart.

—◦◦◦—

Precious Jesus, all around me are people whom I care deeply for and who desperately need to come to know You, but they don't even realize it. May You work in my life so powerfully that they might see something of Your Spirit and be drawn to You. Amen.

NEW LIFE

—◦◦◦—

*In reply Jesus declared, "I tell you the
truth, no one can see the kingdom of God
unless he is born again." "How can a man be born
when he is old?" Nicodemus asked. "Surely he
cannot enter a second time into his mother's womb
to be born!" Jesus answered, "I tell you the truth,
no one can enter the kingdom of God unless
he is born of water and the Spirit."*
—John 3:3–5

Here we are told that men are born of the
Spirit, or born anew through the Holy Spirit's
power. Exactly the same truth is set forth in
Titus 3:5: "He saved us, not because of righ-
teous things we had done, but because of his
mercy. He saved us through the washing of
rebirth and renewal by the Holy Spirit." It is the
work of the Holy Spirit to renew men, to make
men anew, to regenerate men.

What is regeneration? "God, who is rich in
mercy, made us alive with Christ even when
we were dead in transgressions" (Eph. 2:4–5).
Regeneration is the impartation of life to men
who are morally and spiritually dead because

of their trespasses and sins. Every man and woman and child was born into this world spiritually dead. We are by nature moral and spiritual corpses. In regeneration, the Holy Spirit imparts to us His own life.

Of course, the Word of God is the instrument that the Holy Spirit uses in imparting life. "For you have been born again, not of perishable seed, but of imperishable, through the living and enduring word of God" (1 Pet. 1:23). The mere written Word will not produce the new birth, no matter how faithfully preached or taught, unless the Spirit of God makes it a living thing in the hearts of those to whom it is given. This comes out plainly in 2 Corinthians 3:6: "The letter kills, but the Spirit gives life." What did Paul mean? He had just contrasted the Word of God written on parchment with pen and ink to when it is written by the Spirit of God on the hearts of men. The Word written or printed in a book kills, brings condemnation and death; but that Word written by the Spirit in our hearts brings life. It is only the Holy Spirit who can take the heart of the individual and write the Word of God into his heart, making him alive.

—⁓⁓⁓—

Heavenly Father, I know how utterly impossible it is save myself. Only by the miracle of Your life transforming my soul can I be saved. By Your Spirit and Word, may Your life fill my innermost being and continue to shape me in the image of Your Son. Amen.

OUR DESPERATE NEED

——⚬⚬⚬——

*His divine power has given us everything we
need for life and godliness through our knowledge
of him who called us by his own glory and
goodness. Through these he has given us his very
great and precious promises, so that through them
you may participate in the divine nature and escape
the corruption in the world caused by evil desires.*
—2 Peter 1:3–4

Peter tells us that God's definition of regeneration is the impartation of a new nature, "the divine nature," God's own nature, to us.

We are all born into this world with a corrupt nature: corrupt in its thoughts, corrupt in its affections, corrupt in its will.

First of all, every one of us, no matter how fine our ancestry, are born into this world with a mind that is blind to the truth of God. "The man without the Spirit does not accept the things that come from the Spirit of God, for they are foolishness to him, and he cannot understand them, because they are spiritually discerned" (1 Cor. 2:14).

In the second place, we are all born into this world with affections that are corrupt, with affections set upon things that displease God. We love the things we ought to hate, and we hate the things we ought to love.

In the third place, we are all born with a will that is perverse. "The sinful mind is hostile to God. It does not submit to God's law, nor can it do so" (Rom. 8:7). This sinful mind includes a will that is perverse, set upon pleasing self and not upon pleasing God. What pleases self may not be something corrupt or criminal or immoral. What pleases us may be something refined, something of high character; it may not be getting drunk or stealing or lying; it may be culture or music or art or something refined. But pleasing self is the very essence of sin, whether the thing that pleases self is something very high or something very low. Any will that is set upon pleasing itself is a will in rebellion against God. There is only one right attitude for the human will, and that is an attitude of absolute surrender to God, and the whole aim of life should be to please God in all things.

—————

Spirit of God, these words are all true concerning my life. I have loved what I should have hated, my will has been totally bent toward what pleases me, and my mind is blind to Your truth. Break through with Your light and power and set me free. Amen.

SPIRITUAL REBIRTH

—◦◦◦—

*Therefore, if anyone is in Christ, he is a new
creation; the old has gone, the new has come!*
—2 Corinthians 5:17

What occurs in the new birth? We are given
a new nature.

We are given a new mind, a new intellectual nature that instead of being blind to the
truth of God is open-eyed to the truth of God.
Countless times I have seen thoroughly dark-
ened minds become illuminated by the Holy
Spirit in a moment's time, and spiritual truths
long considered foolishness are suddenly as
clear as day.

We are given a new affectional nature as
the Holy Spirit transforms us. We get new tastes
instead of the old tastes, new loves instead of
the old loves. Instead of loving the things that
displease God, we now love what pleases God.
The things we once hated we now love, and
the things we once loved we now hate.

We are also given a new volitional nature,
that is, we are given a new will. When one is

born again of the Spirit, his will is no longer set upon pleasing self: his will is set upon pleasing God. There is nothing else in which he so delights as in the will of God. What he himself desires is nothing to him: what pleases God is everything to him.

The new birth is the impartation of God's own nature into men who are dead in their trespasses and sins. It is the Holy Spirit who imparts this nature. Just as we are utterly dependent upon the work of Christ for us in justification, so we are utterly dependent upon the work of the Holy Spirit in us for regeneration. The whole work of regeneration can be described in this way: the human heart is the soil, the Word of God is the seed, and believers are the sowers. Believers go to the granary of the Bible and take from it that portion of seed they wish to sow; they preach or teach or speak to someone about it; but if it all stopped there there would be no new birth. But if they look to the Holy Spirit to do His work while they sow the Word, He will quicken the seed as it is sown, and it will take root in the hearts of those who listen, and the human heart will close around it by faith, and a new creation will be the result.

—◊◊◊—

God, You are awesome in Your power to transform our lives. There is no miracle that compares to the miracle of the new birth. How I praise You for working in my life, and for saving me from eternal death and corruption. Amen.

THE ONLY WAY

———✿✿✿———

No one who is born of God will continue to sin,
because God's seed remains in him; he cannot go
on sinning, because he has been born of God.
—1 John 3:9

I am often asked if I believe in sudden conversion. I believe in something far more wonderful than sudden conversion. I believe in sudden regeneration. Conversion is an outward thing; it means merely turning around: one is faced away from God, then turns around and faces God. That is conversion. But regeneration goes down to the very depths of the human heart and spirit. It is a radical transformation of the innermost man by the impartation of spiritual life. An outward conversion, if it is to be real and lasting, must be the result of an inward regeneration. A man may be converted a hundred times, but he can be born again but once; for, when one is born again, receiving God's own nature, "God's seed remains in him." Yes, I believe in sudden regeneration, a sudden, thorough transformation of the inmost man.

The new birth is a glorious doctrine that sweeps away false hopes. It comes to the man who is trusting in his morality and tells him that morality is not enough. The man who is trusting in reform, in turning over a new leaf, is told he must be born again. Education and culture, amiability of character, kindness of heart and generosity of giving, trusting in the externals of religion and partaking of the Lord's Supper—none of these are enough. "You must be born again."

But while it sweeps away all false hopes, it also tells you of a better way, the only way. Whether one is down in sin of one kind of another, struggling hard but futilely to break away from sin, or if one has wandered far from God and committed so many sins that he thinks there is no hope, the way is clear: Jesus says you may be born again. The Spirit of God is able and He is ready to make you all over, to impart to you His own nature through His Word, if you will only let Him do it.

———

Son of God, how foolish we are when we try to make ourselves over, try to break the power of sin in our lives, or try to do good and be good in order to gain the Father's acceptance. Thank you for sweeping away these false hopes and showing me the way through the new birth. Amen.

FULLY AND FOREVER SATISFIED

—⚬⚬⚬—

"But whoever drinks the water I give him will never thirst. Indeed, the water I give him will become in him a spring of water welling up to eternal life."
—John 4:14

There is matchless music in these words of Jesus. They are words that held a fascination for me like almost no other utterance of our Lord. They seemed to me like a marvelous strain of music from some far away, heavenly world. And as I came to understand their meaning and to experience for myself the great truth they set forth, there was in them a preciousness that I cannot put into words.

Jesus spoke these words to the Samaritan woman when he was extremely weary and thirsty. Desiring to draw her into spiritual life, Jesus pointed down to Jacob's ancient well and said, "Everyone who drinks this water will be thirsty again" (vs. 13). And how true it is of every earthly fountain of satisfaction or joy; no matter how deeply one drinks, he soon thirsts again. Drink as deeply as you will of the fountain of wealth, you are not satisfied long. Drink of worldly fame or honor or power, but how long will you be content? Drink of worldly pleasures, you will soon want to drink again, only deeper next time. Drink as deeply as you will of the fountain of human knowledge, science, philosophy, literature, music, or art, and you will thirst again. Yes, drink even of that most nearly divine of all human fountains, the fountain of human love, and you soon thirst again. Not one of these things fully satisfies, neither do they satisfy for long.

Then our Lord added the wonderful words that if you drink of the water He gives, the Holy Spirit (John 7:37–39), you will be fully and forever satisfied. I wish that you would sit and ponder these words in silence until their full meaning and full force take entire possession of your mind and heart. Anyone who really receives the Holy Spirit as an indwelling presence will be fully and forever satisfied, and that is the only possible way to be fully and forever satisfied.

—∽∾∿—

Lord Jesus, only You could speak this amazing promise and make the words credible to our hearts. I know something of how unsatisfying it is to drink of this world's fountains. But only You can make real the promise that the Spirit of God can make me fully and forever satisfied. I come to You for this living water. Amen.

JOY IN
THE HOLY SPIRIT

———✸———

*For the kingdom of God is not a matter
of eating and drinking, but of righteousness,
peace and joy in the Holy Spirit.*
—Romans 14:17

It is a great thing to have your source of joy within your own heart; to have a fountain of joy within, not in your surroundings or circumstances or possessions. A joy based in our surroundings or possessions cannot possibly make us always happy. When our possessions and surroundings are intact, we are happy, but when they are gone we are miserable. We are happy when we are rich, but miserable when poor. We are happy when we are well, but miserable when sick. Happy only when others speak well of us and our friends surround us, but plunged into the depths of despair when something changes.

But if our source of joy is in our own hearts, a fountain springing up within us, then we are entirely independent of our surroundings and circumstances, our possessions or lack of possessions. We are equally joyful when rich or poor, when things go just right or "dead wrong," when well or sick, when friends are with us or when they depart us through death. Indeed, the joy of the indwelling Spirit of God even wells up within us in the moments of deepest bereavement. In that dark hour that comes, sooner or later, to everyone, when for the last time we look into the face of some dearly loved one lying cold and still in death, what possible comfort is there in anything that this world can give? But from this fountain within us, which the indwelling Spirit has become, gushes up at such a time as that "inexpressible and glorious joy" (1 Pet. 1:8).

Joy in the Holy Spirit, springing up, always springing up, three hundred and sixty-five days in every year, springs up under all circumstances into everlasting life, a fountain that you can take with you wherever you go. If you have this pure crystal spring of the Holy Spirit in your heart, it will make it impossible for you to seek to satisfy your thirst at the green, slimy pools of this world's pleasures. You can know this wondrous joy today. The Lord Jesus stands before you, all unseen, but nevertheless present, holding out the golden goblet that contains the living water, and says, "Drink deeply." Will you?

———*ฅฅ*———

Our Father in heaven, my desire is to have this fountain of joy welling up in my soul through the Holy Spirit. I confess I am far too dependent upon the world for my happiness. I come to You to drink and be filled. Amen.

THE BAPTISM WITH THE HOLY SPIRIT

———◆◆◆———

"Do not leave Jerusalem, but wait for the gift my Father promised, which you have heard me speak about. For John baptized with water, but in a few days you will be baptized with the Holy Spirit."
—Acts 1:4–5

While a great deal is said today concerning the baptism with the Holy Spirit, it is to be feared that there are many who talk about it and pray for it who have no clear and definite idea of what it is. But the Bible gives a perfectly clear view of this wonderful blessing.

The Bible gives us a number of designations for this one experience. Besides the above verse, we read Acts 2:4, where the promise was fulfilled: "All of them were filled with the Holy Spirit." By the comparison of Acts 10:44–47 with Acts 11:15–16, we find the expressions "the Holy Spirit came on all who heard the message" and "gift of the Holy Spirit" and "received the Holy Spirit" are all equivalents to "be baptized with the Holy Spirit."

We also find that the baptism with the Holy Spirit is a definite experience that one may know whether he has received or not. This is clear from our Lord's command to the apostles: "stay in the city until you have been clothed with power from on high" (Luke 24:49). If this clothing with power, this baptism with the Holy Spirit, were not an experience so definite that one could know whether he had received it or not, how could the disciples possibly know when the days of waiting were over and the days to begin their ministry had begun?

The same thing is clear from Paul's definitive question to the disciples in Ephesus: "Did you receive the Holy Spirit when you believed?" (Acts 19:2). Paul evidently expected a definite yes or no for an answer. How else could these disciples answer Paul's question except in a definite manner? In point of fact he got a definite no. These disciples were completely in the dark about the Holy Spirit, but with Paul's instruction they immediately responded and were baptized with the Spirit on the spot. The Bible is absolutely clear about the definiteness of the baptism with the Holy Spirit.

———

Lord Jesus, Your words were unmistakably clear to Your disciples, but have been abused and confused in our day. I ask You to make them clear to my understanding, so that I may discern the truth and embrace it with faith. Amen.

DISTINCT WORKS OF THE HOLY SPIRIT

———ᴄᴧᴧᴏ———

*"Did you receive the Holy Spirit
when you believed?"*
—Acts 19:2

The baptism with the Holy Spirit is a work of the Holy Spirit distinct from his regenerating work. To be born again of the Spirit is one thing, to be baptized with the Holy Spirit is something different, something additional. This is evident from Acts 1:5: "In a few days you will be baptized with the Holy Spirit." The disciples were not as yet baptized with the Spirit, but they were born again. In John 15:3, Jesus had said to these men, "You are already clean because of the word I have spoke to you." It is clear from James 1:18 and 1 Peter 1:23 that to be made "clean" means to be "born again" through the Word of God. Of the disciples, Jesus noted that all had been made clean except for Judas Iscariot (John 13:10–11). But they were not yet baptized with the Holy Spirit.

The same situation was evident in Acts 8:12–16. Here we find a large company of baptized believers, but the record informs us that when Peter and John visited them, "they prayed for them that they might receive the Holy Spirit, because the Holy Spirit had not yet come upon any of them" (vv. 15–16). In as clear and undeniable language as possible, Scripture shows the baptism with the Holy Spirit to be distinct and something additional to being born again. Let us bow to the teaching of the Word of God even if it does not agree with our preconceived theories.

But I should add that one may be baptized with the Holy Spirit at the very moment he is born again. Such was the case of the household of Cornelius (Acts 10:44), and I believe this was meant to be the norm for the church. The Holy Spirit is every believer's privilege and birthright through the crucified, risen, and ascended Savior, and He has poured out this marvelous gift (Acts 2:33). But in a manner similar to the believers at Ephesus (Acts 19), many believers today have not claimed what is rightfully theirs.

———∞∞∞———

Spirit of God, I see the questions I have about Your work are not new ones, but the New Testament believers did get their answers. I ask You to answer mine as well. Make Your Word absolutely clear to my mind and heart that I may take it in. Amen.

DIVERSITY OF GIFTS

———

*"But you will receive power when the
Holy Spirit comes on you; and you will be my
witnesses in Jerusalem, and in all Judea and
Samaria, and to the ends of the earth."*
—Acts 1:8

The baptism with the Holy Spirit is always connected with and is primarily for the purpose of testimony and service. Indeed, there is not one single passage in the Bible where this experience is spoken of where it is not connected with power for service.

The baptism with the Spirit is not primarily for the purpose of making us holy, although apart from the work of the Spirit we can know nothing of holiness. Nor is the Spirit given to make us happy, although there is great joy in the Holy Spirit. He is primarily given to make us useful to God. While some connect endless ecstasies with the Holy Spirit, in a world where men, women, and children are being swept on unsaved to a hopeless eternity, I would rather go my entire life without one single touch of ecstasy or rapture, and have power to do my part to stem this awful tide and save at least some. The baptism of the Holy Spirit makes us useful for God in the salvation of souls.

This power for service will not manifest itself in precisely the same way in each individual. This is developed in length in 1 Corinthians 12, which speaks of the diversity of the gifts, administrations, and workings of the Holy Spirit. The striking point here is that while there is one baptism of the Holy Spirit, there is a wide variety of manifestations of gifts that are given to individuals by the Holy Spirit, according to the line of service to which the person is called. It is a great mistake to think that everyone who is baptized with the Holy Spirit must speak in tongues, or that everyone receives power as an evangelist or a preacher of the Word and in a manner similar to Wesley or Finney or Moody. This is unscriptural thinking and contrary to the diversity of gifts given. The Holy Spirit for His own wise reason imparts to every person a special gift for the special service to which he is called.

——*∞*——

Heavenly Father, I need to hear this over and over. You know how often I compare what I hear the Holy Spirit has done in someone else's life to what He has done in mine. Show me what it is that You are calling me to do, and empower me accordingly. Amen.

A MISTAKEN NOTION

———✍———

There are different kinds of gifts, but the same Spirit.
There are different kinds of service, but the same
Lord. There are different kinds of working, but the
same God works all of them in all men.
—1 Corinthians 12:4–6

The mistaken notion that I see is so prevalent, that everyone who is baptized with the Holy Spirit will have power as an evangelist, leads to three great evils.

First, it leads to the evil of disappointment, and sometimes even to despair. Many believers seek the baptism of the Spirit, meet the conditions of that baptism, and really do receive it. But God has not called them to an evangelist's work, and therefore He does not empower them with the evangelist's gift. The person ends up perplexed and bewildered, wondering whether they have received the baptism, and some will end up in despair.

The second evil is graver than the first: the error of presumption. Many believers whom God has not called to the work of an evangelist or pastor rush into it because he has received, or thinks he has received, the baptism with the Holy Spirit. It is presumed that "all I need to become a pastor is to receive the baptism with the Holy Spirit." This is very far from the truth. He first needs a call from God to that specific work, then he needs such a knowledge of the Word of God that he has something to preach that is worth listening to, and the baptism of the Spirit as well.

The third evil is the worst of all: the mischief of indifference. There are many who know they are not called to the work of preaching. If they think that the baptism with the Spirit simply imparts power to preach, it is a matter of no personal concern to them. We must come to see the truth that while the Spirit imparts power, the way in which that power will be manifested depends upon the work to which God has called us, and no efficient work can be done without it.

We have the right to "desire the greater gifts" (1 Cor. 12:31), but the Holy Spirit is sovereign, and He must determine the final issue. It is ours to put ourselves unreservedly at His disposal for both the gift and the power for serving Him.

———◦◦◦———

Holy Spirit, You are sovereign God in every way, and I place myself before You to do Your will. I open my heart and say that I am willing for whatever You desire for my life and service. I give up all preconceived notions of what that must look like. Amen.

WHO NEEDS THE BAPTISM WITH THE SPIRIT?

———

"I am going to send you what my Father has promised; but stay in the city until you have been clothed with power from on high."
—Luke 24:49

Shortly before Christ was received up into heaven He gave a definitive command that His disciples should not undertake the work to which He had called them until they had received the all-necessary baptism with the Holy Spirit. These men had already received very thorough preparation for the work at hand. They had taken more than a three-year course in the best theological seminary that ever existed upon earth, and in which our Lord was the sole but all-sufficient Teacher. They had been eyewitnesses of His miracles, His death, His resurrection from the dead, and they were about to be eyewitnesses of His ascension. The work before them was simply to go and tell a perishing world what their own eyes had seen and what their own ears had heard from the lips of the Son of God.

Were they not fully prepared? It would seem so to us. But Christ said, "No, you are so utterly unprepared you must sit down until you are clothed with power from on high for that service. When you receive the baptism with the Holy Spirit—and not until then—you will be prepared for this work." If Christ did not permit these men, who had received such a definite and clear calling—if they were withheld from this work without receiving the Spirit, what is it for us to undertake the work to which He has called us until we have received the same?

But this is not all. In Acts 10:38 we read "how God anointed Jesus of Nazareth with the Holy Spirit and power, and how he went around doing good and healing all who were under the power of the devil." When we look into the Gospels for an explanation of these words, we find in Luke 3:21–4:21 that Jesus' entire ministry was filled with the Holy Spirit. If Jesus Christ, who was divine, very God of very God and yet truly man, did not venture upon the ministry for which the Father had sent Him until thus baptized with the Holy Spirit, what is it for us to dare to do it?

—⊸ɷɷɷ⊸—

Lord Jesus, if You needed the fullness of the Holy Spirit in Your life, how much more do I? If the disciples were not prepared for the work to which You had called them, how much less am I? I humbly bow to You with an open heart for serving You. Amen.

WHO CAN HAVE THE BAPTISM WITH THE HOLY SPIRIT?

—⟡—

"And you will receive the gift of the Holy Spirit. The promise is for you and your children and for all who are far off—for all whom the Lord our God will call."
—Acts 2:38–39

The "promise" that Peter refers to is unquestionably the baptism with the Holy Spirit (Acts 2:33). But whom is this gift for? "For you and your children," says Peter to the Jews whom he was immediately addressing and the generations who would follow them. Then looking down all the coming ages of the church's history to Gentile as well as Jew: "and for all who are far off—for all whom the Lord our God will call." The baptism with the Holy Spirit is for every child of God in every age of the church's history. If it is not ours in experiential possession, it is because we have not taken what God has provided for us in our exalted Savior.

What a thrilling thought that God desires each of us to be clothed with power from on high. But that unspeakably joyous thought has its solemn side. If I may be baptized with the Holy Spirit, I *must* be. If I am baptized with the Holy Spirit, then souls will be saved through my instrumentality who would not be saved if I were not so baptized. If then I am not willing to pay the price of this baptism, I am responsible before God for all the souls who might have been saved but were not saved through me.

We may have a very clear call to service, it may be as clear as the apostles had—but the charge is laid upon us, as upon them, that before we begin that service we must be clothed with power from on high. Anyone who is in Christian work of any type who has not received the baptism with the Holy Spirit should stop his work right where he is and not go on with it until he is. Recall that when the power came upon the disciples they accomplished more in one day than they would have accomplished in years if they had gone on in presumptuous disobedience to Christ's charge. The same can be true for us.

———🙠🙠🙠———

Almighty God and Father, it is thrilling to know that You desire to clothe me with Your power, but it is indeed a solemn thought as well. I come to You that I might be equipped to serve You and to be a witness to those whom You want to reach through me. Amen.

WHERE TO BEGIN

———⟡⟡⟡———

"Repent and be baptized, every one of you, in the name of Jesus Christ for the forgiveness of your sins. And you will receive the gift of the Holy Spirit."
—Acts 2:38

The practical question confronts us: how can we obtain the baptism with the Holy Spirit? The Word of God answers this question very explicitly. There is a clear biblical path consisting of seven simple steps, which anyone who will can take. Whoever takes these seven steps will, with absolute certainty, enter into this blessing. This statement may seem very positive, but the Word of God is equally positive regarding its outcome.

The first three steps are brought out with special distinctness in Acts 2:38. The others which are clearly implied in the verse are brought out more clearly by other passages to which we shall refer later.

The first two steps are found in the word *repent*. What does repentance mean? It means to *change your mind*. But a change of mind about what? As determined by the context in this case, the change of mind was primarily about Jesus Christ. Peter brought against his hearers the awful charge that they had crucified Him whom God had made both Lord and Christ. These words were spoken in the power of the Spirit and "cut to the heart." Peter told them that it was time for them to change their minds about Christ. Change from a Christ-crucifying attitude to a Christ-accepting attitude. Accept Jesus as Christ and Lord—this is the first step toward the baptism with the Holy Spirit.

Have you accepted Jesus as Savior? By that I mean, are you trusting completely in the finished work of Jesus Christ on the cross of Calvary, upon His atoning death for us, as the only ground of your acceptance before God? There cannot be a trace of works righteousness in it, as Paul reminds the Galatians of their experience with the Holy Spirit: "Did you receive the Spirit by observing the law, or by believing what you heard?" (Gal. 3:2). The first step toward receiving the baptism with the Holy Spirit is to rest entirely and absolutely upon what Jesus Christ has already done, not on anything we do.

———✧———

Lord Jesus, I do indeed trust in You completely for my salvation. I denounce trusting in anything I have done or ever will do that might give the appearance of meriting the Father's love. You are my only Savior, and in You alone do I trust. Amen.

REPENTANCE

———❧———

*"Repent and be baptized, every one of you, in the
name of Jesus Christ for the forgiveness of your sins.
And you will receive the gift of the Holy Spirit."*
—Acts 2:38

The second step is also found in the word
repent, a change of mind from that attitude
that loves sin and indulges in sin, to that attitude that renounces sin. This is the second
step toward the baptism with the Holy Spirit:
renounce all sin. Here we touch upon one of
the most vital obstacles to receiving the Holy
Spirit. The Holy Spirit is the *Holy* Spirit, and we
must make a clean-cut choice between the
Holy Spirit and *unholy* sin. We cannot have
both. It is at this point that many people fail of
the blessing. They hold on to something in
their inmost hearts that they more or less
know is not pleasing to God.

If we are to receive the Holy Spirit, there
must be a very honest and thorough heart
searching. We cannot do satisfactory searching ourselves; God must do it. If we wish to

receive the Holy Spirit, we should go alone to God and ask Him to search us thoroughly and bring to light anything that displeases Him (Ps. 139:23–24). Then we should wait for Him to do it. Oftentimes it is what we are pleased to call "a small sin" that shuts us out of the baptism with the Holy Spirit. In reality there are no small sins. There are sins about small things, but every sin is an act of rebellion against God, no matter how small it seems.

If there is anything that always comes up when you get nearest to God, that is the thing that should be put away at once. Many of us do things that we have persuaded ourselves are perfectly right, but that every time when we get nearest to God, these things come up to trouble our conscience. These must be dealt with in the light of God.

If, after patient and honest waiting, nothing is brought to light, we may conclude there is nothing of this kind in the way, and proceed to the next steps. But we should not conclude this too quickly. The sin that hinders often appears very small and insignificant.

—∿∿∿—

Spirit of God, You search the depths of God and You search my heart as well. I ask You to bring to light anything in my life that hinders Your fullness, no matter how small it may seem to me. I will stay before the throne of God and listen for Your voice. Amen.

DAY 24

CONFESSION AND OBEDIENCE

———

*"Repent and be baptized, every one of you, in the
name of Jesus Christ for the forgiveness of your sins.
And you will receive the gift of the Holy Spirit."*
—Acts 2:38

It was immediately after Jesus' baptism that the Holy Spirit descended upon Him (Luke 3:21–22). In Jesus' baptism, though himself sinless, He humbled himself to take the sinner's place, and then God highly exalted Him by giving the Holy Spirit and by the audible testimony: "You are my Son, whom I love; with you I am well pleased" (vs. 22). So we must humble ourselves to make an open confession before the world of our renunciation of sin and of our acceptance of Jesus Christ, *by baptism.* This is the third step toward the baptism with the Spirit. Of course, the baptism with the Spirit may precede water baptism as in the case of the household of Cornelius (Acts 10:44–47). But this was evidently an exceptional case and water baptism immediately followed. I have little doubt that there have been believers who did not believe in or practice water baptism—for example, the Quakers—who received the fullness of the Spirit, but the passage before us certainly presents the normal order.

The fourth step is clearly implied in Acts 2:38, but it is brought out more explicitly in Acts 5:32: "We are witnesses of these things, and so is the Holy Spirit, whom God has given to those who obey him." The fourth step is obedience.

What does obedience mean? It is not merely doing one or two things that God commands, or even of doing most of the things, but doing everything He commands. The heart of obedience is the will. The whole essence of obedience is the total surrender of the will to God. It means that I come to God and say, "Heavenly Father, here I am and all I have. You have bought me with a price and I acknowledge Your absolute ownership. Take me and all I have, and do with me whatever You will. Send me where You will; use me as You desire. I surrender myself and all I possess absolutely, unconditionally, forever to Your control and use."

———⟋∽∽⟍———

I say yes to this, Father in heaven. I am willing to confess my allegiance to Jesus Christ in whatever way You desire from me. And I gladly enter into this surrender of my will to You. I am bought with the sacrifice of Jesus, and I delight to obey You as my Father. Amen.

FULL SURRENDER

—⟶∽⟶—

*He who did not spare his own Son, but
gave him up for us all—how will he not also,
along with him, graciously give us all things.*
—Romans 8:32

More people miss the baptism with the Holy
Spirit at the point of an unconditional surrender of the will to God, and more people enter
into it at this point, than at almost any other.
There are many who go a long ways in the
matter of sacrificing for Christ, going even so
far as to become foreign missionaries, who
still stop short of full surrender to God and so
stop short of the blessing. There is absolutely
no use of your praying for the baptism with
the Spirit if you will not surrender your will to
God, holding absolutely nothing back.

In the Old Testament days, it was when the
burnt offering—*whole,* no part held back—
was lain on the altar that "fire came out from
the presence of the LORD" (Lev. 9:24) and
accepted the gift. And it is when we bring ourselves, a *whole* offering, to the Lord and lay

ourselves thus upon the altar that fire comes and God accepts the gift.

Many are afraid to make a full surrender to God because they fear God's will. They are afraid God's will may be something dreadful, some hard thing. Remember who God is: He is infinite love, and absolute surrender to God is simply absolute surrender to infinite love. Is there anything dreaded in that? And God is our Father. God's love is not only wiser than that of any earthly father, but more tender than any earthly mother. "No good thing does he withhold from those whose walk is blameless" (Ps. 84:11). There is nothing to be feared in God's will. God's will will always prove in the final outcome the best and sweetest thing in all God's universe. Lay your will down and look to your Father to baptize you with the Holy Spirit.

——— ✽✽✽ ———

Loving Father, how can we look at the cross of Jesus and still hold a reservation of fear in our heart about Your will for our lives? I would kneel at the foot of His cross until all the reservations melt away. Holy Spirit, meet me at the cross today. Amen.

THIRSTY?

—∿∿—

Jesus stood and said in a loud voice, "If anyone is thirsty, let him come to me and drink. Whoever believes in me, as the Scripture has said, streams of living water will flow from within him." By this he meant the Spirit, whom those who believed in him were later to receive.
—John 7:37–39

Here again we have the first step toward the baptism with the Spirit, namely, faith in Jesus Christ: "whoever believes in me." But we have also a fifth step in the word *thirst,* "if anyone is thirsty." Our Lord Jesus evidently had Isaiah 44:3 in mind when He uttered those words: "For I will pour water on the thirsty land, and streams on the dry ground; I will pour out my Spirit on your offspring, and my blessing on your descendants." Note carefully the words "if anyone is thirsty."

Were you ever really thirsty? I was among the 60,000 troops at Chickamauga Park during the Spanish-American War, and where there was no rain for many days. The air was full of dust thirty feet high day and night, and we ate dust and drank dust and slept dust and dreamt dust, and no water was fit to drink. I know what it means to be thirsty. When a man really thirsts, it seems as if every pore in his body has just one cry: "Water! Water! Water!" And when a man thirsts spiritually, his whole being has just one cry: "The Holy Spirit! The Holy Spirit! The Holy Spirit! O God, give me the Holy Spirit!" Then it is that God pours floods upon the dry ground, pours His Spirit upon us.

Within us there must be an intense desire that arises out of our utter need of power to do effective service for God, that longs for it at any cost. And it may cost you a good deal. It may take you out of a nice home here in America to China or to India or the heart of Africa. And your intense desire must spring for the glory of God and not for your own glory. Acts 8:18–22 records the solemn case of Simon the magician who desired the Holy Spirit out of his unholy desire. Be careful at this point. Get alone with God and ask Him to show you whether you desire the Holy Spirit that you may glorify God as you should.

—*∿∿*—

Spirit of God, I thirst for You in a dry and thirsty land where there is no water. I am as dry as dust apart from You. Purify my heart that my only motive is to glorify God, to serve my King in a manner that is worthy of His great rule. Amen.

BELIEVING PRAYER

———∿∿∿———

*"If you then, though you are evil, know
how to give good gifts to your children, how
much more will your Father in heaven give the
Holy Spirit to those who ask him!"*
—Luke 11:13

The sixth step toward the baptism with the Holy Spirit is to simply ask God for it. Ask God definitely for the definite blessing. With the first five steps behind you, believing prayer is to be offered for the gift of the Holy Spirit.

It is sincerely contended by some that we should not pray for the Holy Spirit. The line of reasoning is that the Holy Spirit was given to the church at Pentecost as an abiding gift, so why pray for what you have already received? While it is true that the Holy Spirit was given to the church as a whole at Pentecost, each individual must still appropriate the gift for himself, and God's way of appropriation is prayer.

But it is argued still further that every believer has the Holy Spirit, and this is certainly true. "And if anyone does not have the

Spirit of Christ, he does not belong to Christ" (Rom. 8:9). But as we have already seen, it is quite possible to have some of the Spirit's presence and work in the heart and yet come short of that special fullness and work known in the Bible as the baptism or filling with the Holy Spirit. Besides, we have the plain, unquestionable utterance of Jesus Christ that we are to ask Him for the Holy Spirit (Luke 11:13). We also have the accounts of Acts 4:31 and 8:14–17, where those who prayed for the Holy Spirit did indeed receive the Holy Spirit.

Against all inferences is this clear teaching of the Word of God, by precept and example, that the Holy Spirit is given in answer to prayer. It was so at Pentecost; it has been so since. Those whom I have met who give most evidence of the Spirit's presence and power in their lives and work believe in praying for the Holy Spirit. It has been the author's unspeakable privilege to pray with many ministers and Christian workers for this great blessing, and later to learn from them of the new power that had come into their service, none other than the power of the Holy Spirit.

———∾∾∾———

Heavenly Father, in the simplest expression of my heart that I know possible, I ask You to baptize me with the Holy Spirit. I bring nothing but my request to you and my faith that You will indeed work in me. Amen.

FAITH

—◦◦◦—

*"Therefore I tell you, whatever you
ask for in prayer, believe that you have
received it, and it will be yours."*
—Mark 11:24

The seventh and last step, in some respect the simplest of all and yet to many the most difficult, is faith. God's most positive and unqualified promises must be appropriated by faith. "But when he asks, he must believe and not doubt, because he who doubts is like a wave of the sea, blown and tossed by the wind. That man should not think he will receive anything from the Lord" (James 1:6–7). Unless we believe the promise and confidently expect God to do what He has so definitely promised to do, our prayer will bring no result. Here is where countless seekers fail: they do not confidently expect the blessing.

But there is a faith that goes beyond expectation, a faith that just puts out its hand and takes the very thing it asks of God—

"believe that you have received it." "This is the confidence we have in approaching God: that if we ask anything according to his will, he hears us. And if we know that he hears us— whatever we ask—we know that we have what we asked of him" (1 John 5:14). In our definite prayer for the Holy Spirit, there is no question as to whether it is the will of God, and therefore we know that He hears our request. Therefore, I know that I have the baptism with the Holy Spirit based upon my simple faith in the Word of God.

Deal with yourself in this matter of the baptism of the Holy Spirit just as you deal with the matter of an assurance of salvation. Based on the Word of God that if we believe in Jesus Christ we have eternal life, whether we feel it or not, so the Holy Spirit. Be sure you have met the conditions, and then simply ask, claim, and act. Whether or not any experience follows, rest assured that there will be some manifestation of the Spirit (1 Cor. 12:7), but every manifestation of the baptism with the Holy Spirit in the New Testament was in new power in service for God, not in power for feelings.

———∽∾∽———

Holy Spirit, so much of this comes back to grasping for feelings and hoping for a certain type of experience. I release all that and stand before You with nothing but Your promise. It is Your will to fill me with the Spirit, and I have received Him as a gift by faith. I await the way You desire to manifest it in my life, but I anticipate my service to You. Amen.

REFILLINGS WITH THE HOLY SPIRIT

—∞∞—

Do not get drunk on wine, which leads to debauchery. Instead, be filled with the Spirit.
—Ephesians 5:18

In Acts 2:4 we read: "All of them were filled with the Holy Spirit." This was the fulfillment of Acts 1:5: "But in a few days you will be baptized with the Holy Spirit." One of those mentioned by name as being filled with the Spirit was Peter. In Acts 4:8 we read: "Then Peter, filled with the Holy Spirit, said to them..." Here Peter experienced a new filling with the Spirit. Again, in verse 31 we read: "After they prayed, the place where they were meeting was shaken. And they were all filled with the Holy Spirit and spoke the word of God boldly." Peter was named as one of this group, so we see that Peter experienced a third filling with the Holy Spirit.

It is evident that it is not sufficient that a person is once baptized with the Holy Spirit. As new needs of service arise, there must be new fillings with the Spirit. The failure to realize this has led to sad and serious results in many believers' service. For each new service for Christ that is to be performed, for each new soul that is to be dealt with, for each new day and each new need of Christian life and service, we should definitely seek a new filling with the Holy Spirit.

I do not deny that there is an anointing that abides (1 John 2:27), nor the permanency of the gifts that the Holy Spirit gives. I simply assert with clear and abundant Scripture proof, to say nothing of proof from experience and observation, that this gift must not be neglected (1 Tim. 4:14), but rather kindled anew or stirred in a flame (2 Tim. 1:6), and that repeated fillings with the Holy Spirit are necessary to continuance and increase of power.

While some may debate whether these new fillings with the Holy Spirit should be called fresh baptisms, it would seem wisest to follow the uniform biblical usage and speak of the experiences that succeed the first baptism with the Holy Spirit as being "filled with the Holy Spirit."

—◦◦◦—

Holy Spirit, it is true that I need You for every new day and for every person and every situation I encounter. You know my weaknesses as well as my strengths, and that on my own I have nothing of spiritual life to give. Fill me again and again. Amen.

HOW SPIRITUAL POWER IS LOST

—◯◯◯—

*[Samson] did not know
that the LORD had left him.*
—Judges 16:20

Any discussion of the baptism with the Holy Spirit and the power that results from it would be incomplete if attention were not called to how spiritual power may be lost.

God withdraws His power from men when they go back on their separation (Num. 6:2; Judg. 16:20). There was a day when Samson turned his back utterly upon the world and its ambitions, its spirit, its purposes. He separated himself to God, and God honored him with the anointing of His Spirit. But if the world recaptures his heart, the Lord leaves him.

Power is lost through the incoming of sin. King Saul wrought a great victory for God (1 Sam. 11:6,11), but then disobeyed (1 Sam. 13:13–14; 15:3–23), and God withdrew His favor and His power. Saul's history is mirrored in many lives of people whom God has once used. Sin has crept in, and the power of God has been withdrawn.

Power is lost through self-indulgence. The person who would have God's power must lead a life of self-denial. There are many things that are not sinful in the ordinary understanding of the word *sin,* but which hinder spirituality and rob men of power. The gratification of the flesh and fullness of the Spirit do not mix (Gal. 5:17).

Power is lost through greed for money. It was through this that Judas Iscariot fell from the original apostolic company, and it is the love of money that is the root of all kinds of evil (1 Tim. 6:10). How often have people once known what spiritual power was, but money began to come, and little by little it took possession. Even when money is accumulated honestly, the love of it can absorb a person and shut the Spirit out.

Power is lost through pride. How often has a person become puffed up because God has given him power and used him, and God has been forced to set him aside as a proud man (1 Pet. 5:5).

Power is lost through neglect of prayer and the Word of God. God's power is always linked to prayer and God's Word. How quickly do we run dry through their neglect. Let us return always to spend time on our faces before God.

—*◦◊◦*—

Heavenly Father, help me to guard this marvelous gift of Your Holy Spirit. Even in this I will fail if I am left on my own. Whether it's carelessness with sin or a desire for self-indulgence or something else, keep my heart true to You. Amen.